CELEBRATING
FAMILY & FRIENDS
with Fast and Easy MEALS

by Daniel Wansten

Celebrating Family & Friends with Fast and Easy Meals

Copyright © 2025 by Daniel Wansten

For more about this author, please visit https://www.danielwansten.com/

1. Main category—Nonfiction › Cooking, Food & Wine › Meals › Courses & Dishes
2. Other category—Nonfiction › Cooking, Food & Wine › Regional & International › International
3. Other category—Nonfiction › Cooking, Food & Wine › Special Occasions › Party Planning

Published by American Real Publishing
Binghamton, NY
americanrealpublishing.com

Table of Contents

Table of Contents

Table of Contents

Table of Contents

Table of Contents

Table of Contents

Table of Contents

Table of Contents

Introduction

WELCOME TO MY KITCHEN! I BEGAN MY CULINARY JOURNEY AT THE AGE OF FIVE, LEARNING FROM MY GRANDMOTHER AND MOTHER.

Cooking is not just a skill; it's a passion that unveils a world of flavors and experiences on your palate. Just as a stunning piece of artwork captivates viewers and great architecture shapes communities, food has the power to leave a profound impact.

Through my travels from Buenos Aires to northern Canada, and across Europe, the United States, and Asia, I've uncovered incredible recipes that my family has relished. My focus is on crafting fun and easy recipes tailored for busy lives, alongside exciting dishes that are visually stunning and packed with flavor.

Within these pages, you'll discover a treasure trove of culinary delights, from comforting classics to innovative new creations. Each recipe stands as a testament to our collective love for food and the joy it brings to our lives.

This is more than just a cookbook; it's a reflection of my family's story. It embodies the laughter, love, and memories stitched into every dish. Food has an undeniable power to unite us, nourish our bodies and souls, and forge lasting connections.

I invite you to step into my kitchen and embrace the magic of my recipes. Whether you are an experienced cook or just starting out, these recipes will inspire you to create delicious meals and share them with those you cherish. Get ready to elevate your cooking and make lasting memories around the table!

Happy cooking!
Daniel Wansten

Cooking Terms

Baste - To brush on or spoon a liquid over food to keep it moist during cooking.

Blanch - To dip in boiling water, then in cold water, in order to cook food partially or in order to remove its skin or peel.

Blend - To combine ingredients of different textures by mixing gently.

Braise - To brown in fat, then add a small amount of liquid, cover, and cook slowly on the stove or in the oven.

Bread - To coat with flour or bread crumbs for frying.

Broil - To cook over or under direct heat.

Crisp - To soak vegetables in cold water until firm or to heat foods until crisp.

Cube - To cut into small, square pieces.

Cut In - To blend ingredients (e.g., flour & shortening) by using 2 knives or a pastry blender.

Dredge - To coat food with flour or crumbs.

Fillet - To remove bones from meat or fish.

Fold - To combine ingredients with a gentle folding motion.

Fry - To cook in fat in a shallow pan.

Julienne - To cut into long, thin strips.

Knead - To work dough by repeatedly pushing with the heel of the hand and folding over until smooth.

Marinate - To soak food in a liquid to add flavor or to tenderize it.

Mince - To cut into very fine pieces.

Parboil - To boil in water until partially cooked.

Pare - To remove skin; to peel.

Poach - To cook in a hot liquid just below boiling point.

Puree - To put food through a coarse sieve to make a paste or thick liquid from it.

Roux - A mixture of fat and flour, sautéed together, then added to a liquid to thicken it.

Sauté - To fry in a small amount of fat.

Scald - To heat a liquid until hot, but not boiling.

Score - To make shallow cuts in the surface of a food, especially meat.

Skim - To remove the fat that rises to the surface of soup, stew, or gravy by using a spoon or bulb baster.

Steam - To cook food by placing it in a covered, sieve-like container over boiling water.

Steep - To let stand in a hot liquid that is just below boiling temperature.

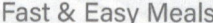

U.S & Metric Measures

Dry Measurements

Measurement	Equipment
1 Lb	16 ounces
1 cup	16 Tbsp
3/4 cup	12 Tbsp
2/3 cup	10 Tbsp plus 2 tsp
1/2 cup	8 Tbsp
3/8 cup	6 Tbsp
1/3 cup	5 Tbsp plus 1 tsp
1/4 cup	4 Tbsp
1/6 cup	2 Tbsp plus 2 tsp
1/8 cup	2 Tbsp
1/16 cup	1 Tbsp
1 Tbsp	3 tsp
1/8 tsp	Pinch
1/16 tsp	Dash
1/2 cup butter	1 stick of butter

Liquid Measurements

Measurement	Equipment
4 quarts	1 gallon
2 quarts	1/2 gallon
1 quart	1/4 gallon
2 pints	1 quart
4 cups	1 quart
2 cups	1/2 quart
2 cups	1 pint
1 cup	1/2 pint
1 cup	1/4 quart
1 cup	8 fluid ounces
3/4 cup	6 fluid ounces
2/3 cup	5.3 fluid ounces
1/2 cup	4 fluid ounces
1/3 cup	2.7 fluid ounces
1/4 cup	2 fluid ounces
1 Tbsp	0.5 fluid ounces

U.S. to Metric Conversions

Measurement	Metric Conversion
Weight Measurements	
1 Lb	454 grams
8 ounces	227 grams
4 ounces	113 grams
1 ounce	28 grams
Volume Measurements	
4 quarts	3.8 liters
4 cups (1 quart)	0.95 liters
2 cups	473 milliliters
1 cup	237 milliliters
3/4 cup	177 milliliters
2/3 cup	158 milliliters
1/2 cup	118 milliliters
1/3 cup	79 milliliters
1/4 cup	59 milliliters
1/5 cup	47 milliliters
1 Tbsp	15 milliliters
1 tsp	5 milliliters
1/2 tsp	2.5 milliliters
1/5 tsp	1 milliliter
Fluid Measurements	
34 fluid ounces	1 liter
8 fluid ounces	237 milliliters
3.4 fluid ounces	100 milliliters
1 fluid ounce	30 milliliters

Oven Temperatures

250°F	120°C
320°F	160°C
350°F	180°C
400°F	205°C
425°F	220°C

Roasting Guide For Meat & Poultry

	Oven Temperature	Cook Time Per Lb.
Beef Rare Medium	325°	20-25 mins.
Well-Done Ham	325°	25-30 mins.
(Precooked) Ham	325°	30-35 mins.
(Uncooked) Pork Loin	325°	15-20 mins.
Lamb Veal	325°	25-30 mins.
	350°	40-45 mins.
	325°	30-35 mins.
	325°	30-35 mins.

	Oven Temperature	Total Cook Time
Chicken (3-4 lbs.)	375°	1 ¾ -2 ¼ hrs.
Chicken breasts	350°	1 ½ hrs.
Turkey (10-14 lbs.)	325°	4-5 hrs.
Duckling (4-5 lbs.)	325-350°	2-3 hrs.
Goose (10-12 lbs.)	325°	4-5 hrs.
Capon (6-8 lbs.)	325-350°	2 ½-3 ½ hrs.

Broiling Guide:

Steaks (1-inch) – 7-10 mins. per side*

Steaks (2-inch) – 10-15 mins. per side*

Chops (1-inch) – 6 mins. per side**

Chops (2-inch) – 10 mins. per side**

Fish (steaks) – 5-7 mins. per side

Fish (fillets) – 6-10 mins. one side only

Rare – 5 inches from heat; well-done – 3 inches from heat **

well-done – 2 inches from heat

Oven & Temperature Chart:

Very Slow – 250-275°

Slow – 275-325°

Moderate – 325-375°

Moderately Hot – 375-400°

Hot – 400-450°

Very Hot – 450-500°

Extremely Hot – 500-525°

Herbs & Spices

Allspice – Pork and ham, pumpkin and squash dishes, gingerbread, sweet baked goods.

Anise – Cookies, cakes, breads.

Basil – Meats, fish and seafood, vegetables, tomato salads and sauces.

Bay Leaf – Meat soups and stews, fish, marinades.

Chervil – Egg dishes, salads and salad dressings, cream sauces, dips.

Chives – Potatoes, soups, salads, dips.

Cinnamon – Middle Eastern meat and rice dishes, toast, quick breads, rice pudding, fruit pies and desserts, tea, cocoa, coffee.

Cloves – Ham, apple desserts, spiced tea.

Dill – Lamb chops, chicken soup, cottage cheese, sauce for fish, potatoes, cucumber salads, coleslaw, carrots, tomatoes, dips.

Garlic – Meat dishes, Chinese-style vegetables, salad dressings, dips, spaghetti sauce.

Ginger – Stir-fried pork or chicken, sweet baked goods, fruit desserts (peach and pear).

Marjoram – Meat soups and stews, fish, dried bean and pea dishes.

Mint – Lamb, fish sauces, peas, cabbage salads, fruit salads, cold drinks.

Nutmeg – Rice dishes, sweet puddings, cauliflower, spinach, mushrooms, eggnog.

Oregano – Roasted meat and poultry, stews, vegetables, salad dressings, tomato sauces, marinades.

Paprika – Meat and poultry, broiled fish, deviled eggs, oven-browned potatoes, potato salad.

Parsley – Poultry, soups and stews, rice, stuffings, potatoes, salad dressings and salads, tomato sauces.

Rosemary – Lamb, pork, veal, poultry.

Sage – Pork, poultry, stuffings, rice.

Tarragon – Roasted poultry, fish, salads and salad dressings.

Thyme – Roasted meats and poultry, soups and stews, fish, stuffings, rice.

Equivalent Amounts

3 tablespoons flour = 1 ounce
3 ½ to 4 cups flour = 1 pound
4 ¾ cups cake flour = 1 pound
2 cups granulated sugar = 1 pound
2 ¼ cups packed brown sugar = 1 pound
4 cups confectioners' sugar = 1 pound (approx.)
2 tablespoons butter = 1 ounce
1 stick butter (½ cup) = 4 ounces
4 sticks butter (2 cups) = 1 pound

4 extra large eggs = 1 cup
5 large eggs = 1 cup
6 medium eggs = 1 cup
7 small eggs = 1 cup
8 to 10 egg whites = 1 cup
12 to 14 egg yokes = 1 cup

1 square unsweetened chocolate = 1 ounce
4 ounces American cheese = 1 cup
shredded 1 package active dry yeast = 1 tablespoon
1 cup unwhipped whipping cream = 2 to 2 ½ cups
whipped 1 pound walnuts in shell = 2 cups shelled
¼ pound chopped walnuts = 1 cup (approx.)

1 cup (½ lb.) uncooked rice = 3 cups cooked (approx.)
1 cup (4 oz.) uncooked macaroni = 2 cups cooked
4 ounces uncooked spaghetti = 2 ½ cups cooked
4 ounces uncooked noodles = 2 ¼ cups cooked

28 saltine crackers = 1 cup fine crumbs
1 slice bread = ¼ cup fine, dry crumbs or ½ cup soft crumbs
22 vanilla wafers = 1 cup fine crumbs
12 graham crackers = 1 cup fine crumbs

Juice of 1 lemon = 3 tablespoons
Juice of 1 orange = ⅓ cup
Grated peel of 1 lemon = 1 teaspoon
Grated peel of 1 orange = 2 teaspoons
1 medium apple, chopped = 1 cup
1 medium onion, chopped = ½ cup
2 stalks celery, chopped = 1 cup
3 to 4 medium potatoes = 1 pound

Substitutions

1 cup sifted all-purpose flour = 1 cup + 2 tablespoons sifted cake flour

1 tablespoon cornstarch (for thickening) = 2 tablespoons flour

1 teaspoon baking powder = ¼ teaspoon baking soda + ½ teaspoon cream of tartar

1 cup granulated sugar = 1 ¾ cups confectioners' sugar

1 cup butter or margarine = ⅞ to 1 cup vegetable shortening or lard + ½ teaspoon of salt

1 cake compressed yeast = 1 package or 2 teaspoons active dry yeast

1 square (1 ounce) unsweetened chocolate = 3 tablespoons cocoa + 1 tablespoon butter

1 whole egg = 2 egg yolks + 1 tablespoon water

1 cup milk = ½ cup evaporated milk + ½ cup water

1 cup sour milk = either 1 cup buttermilk or 1 tablespoon lemon juice or white vinegar + sweet milk to equal 1 cup (let stand 5 minutes)

1 cup sweet milk = 1 cup sour milk or buttermilk + ½ teaspoon baking soda

1 cup heavy (40%) cream = ¾ cup milk + ⅓ cup butter or margarine (do not use for whipping)

1 cup light (20%) cream = ⅞ cup milk + 3 tablespoons butter or margarine

1 cup dairy sour cream = 1 tablespoon lemon juice + evaporated milk to make 1 cup

1 tablespoon prepared mustard = 1 teaspoon dry mustard

1 cup ketchup or chili sauce = 1 cup tomato sauce + ½ cup sugar and 2 tablespoons vinegar (for use in cooked mixtures)

1 teaspoon dried herb leaves = 1 tablespoon chopped fresh herbs

1 garlic clove = 1 teaspoon garlic salt or 1/8 teaspoon powdered garlic

1 small onion = 1 tablespoon instant minced onion

SAUCES & DRESSINGS

Ingredients

- 1 cup salad oil
- ⅓ cup vinegar
- 1 tsp. sugar
- ½ tsp. salt
- ½ tsp. celery salt
- ¼ tsp. dry mustard
- ¼ tsp. cayenne
- 1 clove garlic, minced
- Dash of hot pepper sauce

Instruction

1. Combine ingredients in a jar. Cover and shake. Makes 1⅓ cups.

Homemade Italian Dressing

Ingredients

- ½ cup real mayonnaise
- ¼ cup pickle relish Dash of lemon
- 1 tsp. dill weed

Instruction

1. In a mixing bowl, combine all ingredients. Chill and serve with fish.

Easy Tartar Sauce

Ingredients

- 4 cups water
- 2 tbsp. bouillon (granules or powder)
- 3 tbsp. cornstarch

Instruction

1. Boil water in a pot with the bouillon, then lower to medium-
2. In a measuring cup, put cornstarch in ½ cup cold water. Mix.
3. Pour mixture into the water with bouillon. Stir until the mixture is at medium (or desired) thickness.

Flawless "Gravy"

Ingredients

- Cognac
- Beef broth/stock
- Small container of heavy whipping cream
- Whole black peppercorns

Instruction

1. Fry the steak to your taste, then remove it and let rest while you make the sauce
2. In the fry pan you used to cook your steak, add cognac (1 shot per steak). Simmer rapidly for 1 minute or until the smell of the alcohol is gone.
3. Add beef broth/stock (1 shot per steak) and simmer rapidly.
4. Stir in the heavy whipping cream. Add whole black peppercorns. Stir until the sauce thickens.
5. Serve with steak, potatoes, and sautéed mushrooms

Dad's Creamy Peppercorn Sauce

Dad's note: This is an exceptionally simple sauce with very few ingredients. The perfect way to handle a busy day with a wonderful meal. Delicious over ribeyes or steaks.

Ingredients

- 2 tbsp butter
- 1 tbsp olive oil
- 1 cup finely diced sweet onion
- ½ cup finely diced celery
- ½ cup finely diced carrots
- 1 pinch salt
- 1½ lbs ground beef
- 1½ tsp salt
- ⅛ tsp ground nutmeg
- 1 pinch cayenne pepper
- Freshly ground black pepper, to taste
- 1½ cups 2% milk
- ½ cup dry white wine
- 1 can Italian plum tomatoes
- 2 cups water

Instruction

1. Sauté Veggies: Melt butter and olive oil in a pan. Sauté onion, celery, and carrots with a pinch of salt until soft.
2. Cook Beef: Add ground beef, breaking it apart. Cook until browned, then drain excess fat.
3. Season & Simmer: Stir in salt, nutmeg, cayenne, and black pepper. Pour in milk and let it absorb.
4. Add Wine & Tomatoes: Stir in white wine, cooking until it reduces. Crush tomatoes and add them along with water.
5. Slow Cook: Simmer on low for 2-3 hours, stirring occasionally. Adjust seasoning if needed.

Bolognese Sauce

BREAKFAST

Ingredients

- 3 large potatoes (peeled)
- ½ sweet yellow onion (diced)
- Salt & pepper, to taste
- ¼-½ stick butter

Instruction

1. In a strainer, grate potatoes. Rinse well with water to get out as much starch from potatoes as you can.
2. Once drained, place hashbrowns in a skillet with butter over medium heat. Add onions, salt, and pepper to taste.
3. Brown hashbrowns on both sides well and serve.

Homemade Hashbrowns

Ingredients

- 3 tbsp. butter, melted 1 medium
- sweet yellow onion, diced 1
- 20oz. bag frozen hash brown potatoes
- 1 10oz. can cream of mushroom soup
- 1 cup regular sour cream
- 2 cups shredded cheddar cheese
- 2 tsp. garlic salt
- 1 cup chicken broth

Instruction

1. Preheat the oven to 350°.
2. Rub cooking oil in the bottom and sides of a 9x13 baking
3. In a large mixing bowl, add all ingredients together. (Save ½ cup of the cheddar cheese to sprinkle on top before baking.) Make sure the butter is melted! Stir until well mixed.
4. Spread mixture into prepared baking dish. Sprinkle the remaining ½ cup of cheese evenly over the top.
5. Put in oven and bake for 30-40 minutes, or until lightly golden brown. Serve!

Dreamy Cheesy Hash Brown Potato

Ingredients

- For Muffins:
- English muffins (1 per serving) Thinly sliced ham Poached egg (1 per serving)
- For Hollandaise sauce:
- 4 egg yolks
- ½ cup butter, cut in thirds
- 2-3 tsp. lemon juice Salt White pepper

Instruction

1. Whip all ingredients (except butter) together.
2. Melt butter in small pan.
3. Pour egg mixture into the heated, buttered pan. Using a rubber spatula, turn eggs over constantly on medium heat. Eggs should be moist and fluffy, never brown.
4. Serve with an english muffin.

Daniel's "Magic Eggs"

Ingredients

- Ingredients 6 eggs, whipped until fluffy
- ½ cup ricotta cheese, whipped in with eggs
- 1 oz. sweet yellow onion
- 1 oz. bacon bits
- 1 slice of Canadian bacon, diced
- 10 spinach leaves
- ¼ stick European butter

Instruction

FOR MUFFINS:
1. For each serving, split and toast one english muffin.
2. Top with thin slices of ham and one poached egg.
3. Prepare hollandaise sauce and pour over prepared muffin.

FOR HOLLANDAISE SAUCE:
1. Place egg yolks and ⅓ butter in a pan. Cook until butter melts, stirring rapidly.
2. Add ⅓ more of the butter and continue stirring.
3. As mixture thickens and butter melts, add the remaining butter. Stir constantly
4. Add lemon juice, salt, and white pepper. Thicken, stir, and remove from heat. Serve.

Eggs Benedict

Ingredients

- 1 ¼ cups sifted all purpose flour
- 3 tsp. baking powder (for fluffier pancakes, add 3 more tsp.)
- 1 tbsp. sugar
- ½ tsp. salt
- 1 egg, beaten
- 1 cup milk
- 2 tbsp. salad oil

Instruction

1. Mix dry ingredients together well.
2. Add wet ingredients to dry ingredients, stirring until mixture is moistened like a batter.
3. Bake batter on a hot griddle. Makes 12 pancakes.

Homemade Pancakes

Ingredients

- ¼ cup sugar
- 1 tsp. ground cinnamon
- 2 tbsp. butter, melted flour cream cheese frosting frozen roll of dough (or dough made from scratch)

Instruction

1. Roll dough out on a lightly floured surface.
2. Mix sugar and cinnamon. Add the butter, then spread the mixture over dough.
3. Roll into a jelly roll, starting with the long edge. Seal.
4. Cut into 1-inch slices. Place on a greased baking pan. Cover.
5. Let the roll rise in a warm place until it doubles in size, or about 30-45 minutes.
6. Bake at 375° for 20 minutes.
7. Remove from the pan and frost with cream cheese frosting. Makes 16 rolls.

Homemade Cinnamon Rolls

APPETIZERS & DIPS

Ingredients

- 1 3 oz. package cream cheese, softened
- 1 tbsp. pimiento-stuffed green olives, chopped
- 1 tsp. grated onion
- ¼ tsp. dried dill weed
- dash of salt
- 1-2 tbsp. light cream

Instruction

1. Combine cream cheese, olives, onion, dill weed, and salt.
2. Stir in cream to make a mixture of dipping consistency. Chill and serve. Makes about ⅔ cup of dip.

Vegetable Dill Dip

Ingredients

- ¾ cup mayonnaise
- 1½ cups sour cream
- 1½ tsp. onion powder
- ½ tsp. garlic powder
- ½ tsp. paprika
- 2 tsp. worcestershire sauce
- 1 tsp. fresh lemon juice
- 1½ tsp. kosher salt
- ½ tsp. fresh ground black pepper
- 3 green onions, finely diced
- 1 8oz. can water chestnuts, drained & finely diced
- 2 10oz. packages frozen chopped spinach, thawed & squeezed dry
- ½ cup carrots, shredded & chopped
- salt & pepper, to taste

Spinach Dip

Instruction

1. In a large bowl, add mayo, sour cream, onion powder, garlic powder, paprika, worcestershire sauce, lemon juice, salt, and pepper. With a hand whisk, mix well.
2. Add green onion, water chestnuts, carrots, and spinach to bowl. Stir thoroughly.
3. Cover and refrigerate at least 2 hours.
4. Serve in a sourdough bread bowl with breadcrumbs and assorted vegetables.

Ingredients

- 8 oz. cream cheese
- ½ cup mayo
- ½ cup sour cream
- 2 cups chopped marinated artichoke hearts, drained
- 1 cup grated parmesan cheese
- ½ tsp. garlic powder

Instruction

1. Preheat oven to 350°. With a hand mixer, cream together cream cheese, mayo, and sour cream.
2. Add the remaining ingredients and mix well. Spoon the mixture onto a greased 9x13 baking dish.
3. Bake at 350° for 25-30 minutes, or until slightly browned. Serve with crackers or tortilla chips.

Artichoke Dip

(The Best Hot Artichoke Dip!)

Ingredients

- 2 cans diced tomatoes
- medium sweet yellow onion, diced
- ½ tsp. salt
- ⅔ tsp. chili powder
- 3 tbsp. cilantro
- 1 tbsp. garlic powder
- ¼ cup lime juice
- 2-4 tbsp. mccormick™ red pepper flakes (adjust according to how hot you like it)

Instruction

1. Mix all ingredients together well.
2. Let marinate for at least 2-3 hours. Serve with tortilla chips.

Salsa

Ingredients

- 4-6 ripened avocados
- 1 ripened tomato, chopped
- 1 fresh lemon
- ½ sweet yellow onion, grated
- 1 tsp. chili powder
- ½ tsp. sea salt
- ½ cup mayo

Instruction

1. Preheat oven to 350°. With a hand mixer, cream together cream cheese, mayo, and sour cream
2. Add the remaining ingredients and mix well. Spoon the mixture onto a greased 9x13 baking dish.
3. Bake at 350° for 25-30 minutes, or until slightly browned. Serve with crackers or tortilla chips.

Mom's Guacamole

Ingredients

- 7 hard-boiled eggs
- ¼ cup mayo
- 1 tsp. vinegar
- 1 tsp. mustard
- salt & pepper

Instruction

1. Halve the hard-boiled eggs lengthwise. Remove the yolks and mash them in a bowl with desired combination of other ingredients.
2. Fill the whites of the boiled eggs with your mixture and serve.

Deviled Eggs

Ingredients

- Deli ham (or other assorted meats)
- 2 bundles of green onion
- 1-2 tubs sour cream

Instruction

1. Take one slice of meat and lay it out on a flat surface.
2. Put green onion on the meat, leaving the tail of the onion out a bit.
3. Put 1 tbsp. Sour cream over the onion and roll the meat around it.
4. Place and arrange multiple hors d'oeuvres on a pretty plate and serve.

Hors d'Oeuvres

Ingredients

- long toothpick-like skewers
- assorted cubed cheeses
- assorted olives

Instruction

1. Arrange olives and cheeses on a skewer.
2. Arrange multiple skewers on a party tray. Chill for 2 hours and serve.

Quick Party Hors d'Oeuvres

Ingredients

- 1 large sweet yellow onion
- flour
- ½ tsp. salt
- 1 slightly beaten egg
- 1 cup milk
- 2 tbsp. salad oil

Instruction

1. Cut onion into ¼ inch slices. Separate the ring into individual pieces.
2. Combine flour, salt, egg, milk, and salad oil in a bowl and mix well.
3. Coat the onion rings with batter. Fry each ring a few minutes at a time in deep (not too hot) vegetable oil.
4. Once the onion rings are golden brown, drain them on a paper towel. Sprinkle each with salt and serve.

Golden Onion Rings

Ingredients

- 4 bagels, sliced in half
- 1 can seasoned basil tomato sauce
- 1 ½ tsp. oregano
- light red pepper flakes
- grated mozzarella
- pepperoni slices

Instruction

1. Place oven on broil.
2. Spread sauce over each bagel half. Sprinkle with oregano and red pepper flakes.
3. Put pepperoni on each bagel and top with cheese.
4. Broil bagels for 6 minutes and serve.

10-Minute Pizza Bagels

SIDES

Ingredients

- 3 cups bread crumbs
- 4 oz. cooked Jimmy Dean® sausage, crumbled
- ¾ cup red Jonathan apple, diced
- ½ cup walnuts, chopped
- ½ tsp. rubbed sage
- 1 tsp. rosemary leaves, crushed
- ¾ cup water
- ⅓ cup butter
- 1 box chicken broth

Instruction

1. Mix together all ingredients, adding chicken broth for flavor.
2. Do not place in turkey, but bake separately in a casserole dish at 350° at 1 ½-2 hours.

American Stuffing

Ingredients

- 1 5lb. bag russet potatoes, peeled & quartered
- 1-2 cups milk
- ½ stick Land-o-Lakes® European style butter

Instruction

1. Put potatoes in a pot of water. Bring to a boil until potatoes are tender, or about 20-25 minutes.
2. Drain, add milk, and mix with an electric mixer on high. Continue adding milk until the potatoes are creamy.
3. Top with ½ stick of butter and serve.

Mom's Mashed Potatoes

Mom's note: The true secret to fluffy mashed potatoes is to use russet potatoes and add milk for extra fluff.

Ingredients

- ·4 cups cauliflower florets
- 1 oz. I Can't Believe It's Not Butter!® spray
- 1 oz. Land O Lakes® gourmet fat free half & half
- Pinch of salt
- Pinch of fresh ground pepper

Instruction

1. Steam or microwave the cauliflower until it's soft.
2. Puree the softened cauliflower in a food processor, adding the butter spray and half & half to taste. Season with salt and pepper.

Surprise South Beach "Mashed Potatoes"

Mom & Dad's note: Absolutely yummy!

Ingredients

- 4-6 large russet potatoes
- Extra virgin olive oil
- Sea salt
- Dash of pepper

Instruction

1. Rinse and wash potatoes. Place them on a baking sheet.
2. Rub olive oil, sea salt, and pepper on the potatoes. Poke holes on both sides of each potato with a fork.
3. Bake the potatoes on convection bake at 350°-400° for 1 hour and 15 minutes. Serve with butter and sour cream.

Perfect Baked Potatoes

Ingredients

- 6-8 medium potatoes, pared & thinly sliced (about 6 cups)
- ¼ cup onion, finely chopped
- ½ cup all purpose flour
- 1 ½ tsp. salt
- ⅛ tsp. pepper
- 2 cups milk
- 3 tbsp. buttered fine dry breadcrumbs

Instruction

1. Place half of the potatoes and half of the onion in a greased 2-quart casserole dish. Sift half of the flour over the dish and sprinkle with half of the seasonings.
2. Repeat step 1 for a second layer.
3. Pour milk over the dish. If desired, sprinkle the top with dry breadcrumbs.
4. Cover and bake at 350° for 1 ¼ -1 ½ hours.
5. Uncover and bake for 15 additional minutes. Serves 6.

Homemade Scalloped Potatoes

Ingredients

- 2 cans Del Monte® cut green beans
- 1 can cream of mushroom soup
- ¾ cup milk
- 1 can French's® crispy fried onions
- ¼ tsp. pepper

Instruction

1. Mix all ingredients together in a bowl (saving some of the fried onions for a topping).
2. When everything is mixed together well, place in a casserole dish. Top with remaining onions.
3. Bake at 350° for 45 minutes.

Green Bean Casserole

Ingredients

- Fresh Brussels sprouts
- 1-2 tbsp. real butter
- Salt & pepper, to taste
- Dash of light fresh garlic

Instruction

1. Clean and cut brussels sprouts in half.
2. In a large skillet, add butter and turn on medium-low heat.
3. Place brussels sprouts in the skillet. Season with remaining ingredients and toss until golden brown.

Sautéed Brussels Sprouts

Mom & Dad's note: So amazing!

Ingredients

- 1 large can black beans (with sauce)
- 1 garlic clove, finely grated or pulverized
- 1 tbsp chili powder (adjust to taste)
- 2-3 shakes red pepper flakes
- 1 chicken bouillon cube, dissolved in ¼ cup hot water
- 1 sweet onion, diced
- ½ stick European butter
- ¼ poblano pepper, finely diced
- 1 tbsp butter (for sautéing)
- Mozzarella cheese (for serving, optional)

Instruction

1. Prepare the black beans:
   - Pour the black beans (with sauce) into a pot.
   - Heat over medium heat and cover, allowing the beans to soften.
2. Season the beans:
   - Add the grated or pulverized garlic.
   - Stir in chili powder, red pepper flakes, and the dissolved chicken bouillon.
3. Sauté the onion and peppers:
   - In a separate pan, melt 1 tbsp butter over medium-low heat (do not brown the butter).
   - Add the diced sweet onion and cook until softened but not translucent.
   - Add the european butter and diced poblano pepper.
   - Sauté until everything softens and flavors meld.
4. Combine & simmer:
   - Add the sautéed onion and poblano mixture to the black beans.
   - Stir well and let simmer on low heat for 20-30 minutes, stirring often to prevent burning.

Daniel's Black Bean Dip or Side

SALADS

Ingredients

- Strawberries
- Blueberries
- Blackberries
- Kiwi
- Pineapple
- Mandarin Oranges
- Bananas
- Green Grapes
- Red Grapes
- Apple
- 1 tbsp. lemon juice
- 1 tbsp. honey
- (If you like, you can use vanilla pudding to replace lemon juice and honey)

Instruction

1. Cut up all fruit and rinse in cold water.
2. Place fruit into a large mixing bowl. Add honey and lemon (or vanilla pudding) and toss throughout the fruit.
3. Chill and serve.

Fruit Salad

Ingredients

- 1 package fresh baby spinach, rinsed
- Sliced strawberries (you judge the amount, but not too heavy is best)
- (You may also use cherries, raspberries, or other fruits based on preference)
- Feta cheese, crumbled lightly
- ½ cup walnuts, chopped
- Vinaigrette dressing (matched according to fruit used—If strawberries are used, use strawberry vinaigrette. If raspberries are used, use raspberry vinaigrette, etc.)

Instruction

1. Put spinach in a large salad bowl. Sprinkle the rest of the ingredients on top.
2. Add salad dressing that correlates with which fruit you used. Mix well.
3. Chill for 1 hour. Serve.

Strawberry Spinach Salad

Ingredients

- 2 cucumbers, cleaned and diced into cubes
- 2 quarts cherry tomatoes, cleaned and sliced into halves
- ½ Bermuda onion, sliced thinly and cut into halves
- 2-3 ripe avocados, peeled, seed removed, & diced into small cubes
- Paul Newman's Italian Family Recipe salad dressing

Instruction

1. In a large mixing bowl, add cucumbers, tomatoes, onion, and avocados. Toss together.
2. Add dressing to taste. Chill and serve.

Cucumber Tomato Avocado Salad

Ingredients

- 2 cups spring mix salad
- 2 cups baby spinach
- 3 slices cooked/fried bacon, crumbled (do not burn!)
- 2 tbsp. extra virgin olive oil
- 1 tbsp. red wine vinegar
- ⅛ tsp. kosher salt
- ⅛ ground red pepper
- 1½ tsp. fresh oregano, chopped
- 2½ tsp. toasted pine nuts
- 2 tbsp. feta cheese, crumbled
- ½ cup walnuts, chopped
- ½-¾ cups Kalamata olives
- Girard's Champagne Dressing

Instruction

1. Place the spring mix and spinach into a large salad bowl. Mix.
2. In a separate bowl, mix red wine vinegar, salt, pepper, and oregano. Pour mixture over spring mix and spinach salad. (You may use champagne dressing instead if you'd like.)
3. Take pine nuts and roast them in a fry pan on the stove. (This takes about 5 minutes.) Do not burn them. When the nuts are roasted, pour them over the salad.
4. Add the remaining ingredients to the mix: peppers, olives, bacon, feta cheese, and walnuts.
5. Chill for 1 hour and serve.

Roasted Red Pepper Pine Nut Salad

Ingredients

- 8 large potatoes (russet is best)
- 1½ cup mayo
- 1½ tbsp. mustard (or amount for desired taste)
- 3 stalks celery, finely chopped
- 1 tsp. celery salt

Instruction

1. Boil potatoes—with skin on—for about 20 minutes, or until tender. Let cool.
2. In a separate bowl, add mustard, mayo, celery, and celery salt. Mix well.
3. Peel cooled potatoes and dice them into large pieces. Place potatoes in a large bowl with all other ingredients. Mix well.
4. Cover, chill, and serve.

Potato Salad

Ingredients

- 2 cups imitation crab meat, shredded
- 2 cups cooked shrimp, chopped
- 1 stalk celery, chopped
- 1 cup celery salad mix (or extra chopped celery)

Dressing:
- 1 cup mayonnaise
- 1 tablespoon cream (to thin the dressing)
- 1 ½ teaspoons dill weed

Seafood Salad

Instruction

1. In a large bowl, combine the crab meat, shrimp, chopped celery, and celery salad mix.
2. In a separate bowl, mix the mayonnaise with a touch of cream until smooth. Stir in the dill weed.
3. Pour the dressing over the seafood mixture and toss gently until well coated.
4. Serve chilled and enjoy!

Ingredients

Salad:
- 6 cups broccoli florets (about 2.5 heads of fresh broccoli)
- ⅔ cup raisins
- ⅔ cup bacon, cooked and chopped
- ½ cup slivered almonds

Dressing:
- 1 cup mayonnaise (or substitute with a touch of cream or milk for a creamier texture)
- 1½ tbsp white vinegar
- 2 tbsp sugar
- Dash of salt
- Dash of pepper

Instruction

1. In a large bowl, combine the broccoli florets, raisins, bacon, and slivered almonds.
2. In a separate bowl, whisk together the mayonnaise (or cream/milk), white vinegar, sugar, salt, and pepper until smooth.
3. Pour the dressing over the broccoli mixture and toss until everything is well coated.
4. Serve immediately or chill for 30 minutes to allow the flavors to meld.

Broccoli Salad

Ingredients

- 1 package (1 lb or 450g) arugula or spring mix salad
- 1 jar (about 12 oz or 340g) roasted red peppers, drained and sliced
- ½ cup feta cheese, crumbled
- ½ cup Kalamata olives, pitted and sliced
- ½ cup roasted pine nuts
- ½ cup Champagne vinaigrette dressing

Instruction

1. In a large salad bowl, combine the arugula or spring mix, roasted red peppers, feta cheese, kalamata olives, and roasted pine nuts.
2. Drizzle with Champagne vinaigrette dressing and toss gently to coat all ingredients evenly.
3. Cover and chill in the refrigerator for about 15–20 minutes to let the flavors meld.
4. Serve fresh and enjoy!

Pine Nut Salad (Arugula)

Ingredients

- 1 package (approx. 5 oz) baby spinach
- ¾ cup strawberries, sliced (or any other fruit of choice)
- ½ cup feta cheese, crumbled
- 1 cup walnuts, chopped
- ½ cup vinaigrette dressing (strawberry or another flavor of choice)

Instruction

1. Prepare the ingredients: wash and dry the baby spinach leaves. Slice the strawberries or other fruit.
2. Assemble the Salad: In a large bowl, combine the spinach, sliced strawberries, crumbled feta cheese, and walnuts.
3. Dress the Salad: Drizzle the vinaigrette over the salad and gently toss to coat everything evenly.
4. Serve and Enjoy: Transfer to a serving plate and enjoy as a fresh, healthy dish!

Baby Spinach /Feta Vinaigrette Salad

SOUPS & STEWS

Ingredients

- 6 chicken thighs, with skin on
- 1 sweet yellow onion
- ½ jar chicken bouillon
- 1 box chicken broth
- 1 large package mixed veggies
- 1 small package sweet peas

For drop noodles:
- 8-10 eggs
- 3-4 cups flour

Instruction

1. Cut shrimp in half and chop up crab meat.
2. Place shrimp and crab into a mixing bowl, along with remaining ingredients, and mix well.
3. Cover and chill for 2-3 hours, then serve.

Chicken & Spaetzle Soup

Ingredients

- 1-2 packages beef stew meat
- 1 sweet yellow onion
- 1-2 garlic cloves, chopped
- ½ jar beef bouillon granules
- 1 box beef broth
- 2 tbsp. olive oil
- 2 bay leaves
- 1 can V8 juice
- 2 cans diced tomatoes
- 1 large package mixed vegetables
- 1 package sliced fresh mushrooms
- 2 large potatoes, diced into chunks

Instruction

1. In a large pot, add olive oil, beef, and garlic. When it starts to brown, add 2 tbsp. Beef bouillon with a bit of beef broth to caramelize the mixture.
2. When it caramelizes well, add the onion, mushrooms and a bit more beef broth, continuing to caramelize until it reaches your desired taste.
3. Add the rest of the ingredients to the caramelized meat mix, along with 1-2 cups of water. Cook on medium-low heat for 45 minutes to 1 hour and serve.

Vegetable Beef Soup or Stew

Ingredients

- 2 tbsp. olive oil
- 1 cup onions, chopped
- 2 tsp. garlic, chopped
- 1 poblano chili pepper
- 1 jalapeño pepper, seeded & chopped
- 1½ tsp. salt
- 1½ tsp. cumin
- ½ tsp. coriander
- 1 tbsp. tomato paste
- 6 cups chicken stock
- 1 lb. chicken breast, cooked & cut into cubes
- ¼ cup cilantro, chopped
- 2 tsp. lime juice
- 1 avocado, smashed & diced
- ½ cup sour cream
- 1 tsp. chipotle in adobo sauce

Instruction

1. In a large pot, heat the oil. Add onions, garlic, chili pepper, jalapeño, salt, cumin, and coriander. Cook for 5 minutes, stirring frequently.
2. Add the tomato paste and cook for an additional 1 minute.
3. Add the chicken stock and simmer for 20 minutes.
4. Add the chopped chicken breast and simmer for 5 minutes.
5. Add the cilantro and lime juice, then remove from the heat.
6. Garnish with tortilla chips, avocados, and chipotle and/or sour cream

Tortilla Soup

Ingredients

- 2 lbs. grey peeled shrimp
- 8 oz. uncooked rice
- ½ stick butter
- 2 tbsp. flour
- 1 medium onion, finely chopped
- 1 clove garlic, crushed
- 1 14 oz. can tomatoes
- 4 cups chicken broth
- ¼ tsp. ground ginger
- Pinch of allspice
- Pinch of salt
- Pinch of Tabasco®
- ½ tsp. dried thyme
- ¼ tsp. cayenne pepper
- Green onion, for garnish

Dad's Cabo San Lucas Jambalaya

Instruction

1. In a heavy saucepan, melt butter and add flour. Stir to blend well and cook over low heat until the mixture turns a pale straw color.
2. Add onion, garlic, and red pepper and cook until soft. Add the tomatoes with their juice, steadily breaking up the tomatoes with a fork.
3. Add chicken broth and mix well. Add ginger, allspice, thyme, cayenne pepper, salt, and Tabasco®, then bring to a boil for 2 minutes, stirring rapidly.
4. Add rice, stir well, and cover. Cook for about 20 minutes, or until rice is tender and has absorbed most of the liquid.
5. Add the shrimp during the last 10 minutes of cooking time. Cook until the shrimp curl and turn pink.
6. Spoon into a serving dish and sprinkle with chopped green onion. Serves 2-4.

Ingredients

- 1 cup all purpose flour
- ¾ cup bacon drippings (do not use burned bacon fat)
- 1 cup coarsely chopped celery
- 1 large sweet yellow onion, chopped
- 1 large green bell pepper, chopped
- 2 cloves minced garlic
- 1 lb. Andouille sausage, sliced
- 3 quarts water
- 6 cubes beef bouillon
- 1 tbsp. white sugar
- Salt, to taste
- 2 tbsp. Tabasco® sauce (or ½ tsp. Cajun)
- Dash of Worcestershire sauce
- 4 bay leaves
- ½ tsp. dried thyme leaves
- 1 14.5oz can stewed tomatoes
- 1 6 oz. can tomato sauce
- 2 tsp. gumbo file powder
- 2 10 oz. packages okra (thawed)
- 2 tbsp. distilled white vinegar
- 1 lb. lump crab meat
- 3 lbs. uncooked medium shrimp

Instruction

1. Make the roux: whisk flour and bacon drippings in a saucepan over medium-low heat, stirring constantly until mahogany brown (20-30 min). Remove from heat.
2. Sauté Vegetables & Sausage: Pulse celery, onion, bell pepper, and garlic in a food processor. Stir into roux with sausage and cook for 10-15 min until tender. Set aside.
3. Simmer Base: Boil water and dissolve bouillon cubes in a large pot. Whisk in the roux mixture, then add sugar, salt, hot sauce, Worcestershire sauce, bay leaves, thyme, tomatoes, and tomato sauce. Simmer for 1 hour, adding 2 tsp. gumbo file at the 45-minute mark.
4. Prepare Okra: Cook okra with vinegar in a skillet for 15 min. Remove and stir into gumbo.
5. Add Seafood: Mix in crab, shrimp, and simmer for 45 more min. Just before serving, stir in 2 more tsp. gumbo file. Serve with rice.

New Orleans Creole Gumbo

Ingredients

- 1 can drained white northern or navy beans
- 1 can drained kidney beans
- 1 lb. ground hot Italian sausage
- ½ yellow onion
- 3 tsp. garlic, minced
- 4 cups chicken broth
- 1 15 oz. can tomato sauce
- 1 15 oz. can diced (not drained) tomatoes
- 2 celery ribs, chopped
- ½ cup carrots, julienne style
- 1 cup ditalini pasta, boiled until tender
- 1 tsp. salt
- 1½ tsp. dried Italian blend seasoning
- ¼ tsp. crushed red pepper flakes
- ½ bag spinach
- Freshly-grated parmesan

Instruction

1. Brown the italian sausage.
2. Mix together all ingredients (except spinach and parmesan) and simmer until ready.
3. Toward the end of cooking, add the spinach.
4. Serve with freshly-grated parmesan on top.

Instant Pasta e Fagioli Soup

Ingredients

- 7-10 celery stalks, diced
- 1 white onion (sweet yellow works, too)
- 6 cloves garlic, minced
- 4 tbsp. extra virgin olive oil
- 2 lbs. lean ground beef
- 2 lbs. Jimmy Dean® regular sausage
- 1 tsp. sea salt
- 2 tbsp. oregano
- 2 tbsp. dried basil
- 1 tbsp. cumin
- 3-4 tbsp. chili powder (or more, if needed)
- ½ tsp. cayenne pepper
- 1 16 oz. can diced tomatoes (with juice)
- 8 oz. chicken broth

Instruction

1. In a large soup pot, sauté the veggies in the olive oil for about 1 minute. Add and brown the beef and sausage.
2. Season the meat mixture with all of the spices.
3. Add tomatoes and chicken broth. Simmer for 35 minutes.
4. Taste and add more seasoning as desired.

Paleo Chili

Ingredients

- 2 lbs. lean ground beef
- 2 lbs. Jimmy Dean® original sausage
- 3 28 oz. cans diced tomatoes
- 1 can mushrooms, drained
- 1 can dark kidney beans, drained
- 2 15 oz. cans refried beans, with sausage
- ⅓ container dark chili powder (not Mexican)
- 3 cloves garlic, grated
- ½ large sweet yellow onion
- 1 heaping tbsp. fresh diced poblano pepper (about ½ a pepper)
- 1 tsp. tarragon
- Salt, to taste
- 1 bottle Tostito® Restaurant Style medium salsa

Dad's Chili

Instruction

1. THOROUGHLY BROWN THE GROUND BEEF AND SAUSAGE IN A PAN WITH GARLIC, TARRAGON, ONION, AND LIGHT SALT.
2. Add the meat mixture to a pot with all other ingredients and mix completely. Simmer for 3 hours, stirring every 10 minutes. To avoid burning, bring the bottom of the pot to the top by stirring in a circular motion.
3. Simmer for 20 minutes or until the mixture is thoroughly marinated.
4. Serve with Tostito® chips.

Ingredients

- 1–2 lbs beef stew meat
- 1 yellow sweet onion, chopped
- 1–2 cloves garlic, chopped
- 2 tbsp olive oil
- 2 tbsp beef bouillon
- 1 box beef broth
- 1 can juice
- 2 cans diced tomatoes
- 1 bag mixed vegetables
- 1 pack sliced fresh mushrooms
- 2 large potatoes, diced

Instruction

1. Brown the beef: in a large pot, heat olive oil over medium heat. Add beef and brown. Stir in bouillon and a bit of beef broth to caramelize.
2. Sauté Aromatics: Add onions and garlic, cooking until fragrant.
3. Add Remaining Ingredients: Pour in V8 juice, diced tomatoes, mixed vegetables, mushrooms, potatoes, remaining broth, and 1–2 cups of water.
4. Simmer: Cook on medium heat for 45 minutes to 1 hour, stirring occasionally.
5. Serve & Enjoy!

Vegetable Beef Soup & Stew

SANDWICHES & WRAPS

Ingredients

- 1 long French roll (should be about 24 in.)
- Assorted deli meats: ham, salami, turkey, beef
- American cheese
- Shredded lettuce
- Sliced tomatoes
- Sweet yellow onion, thinly sliced
- Salt & pepper, to taste
- Mayo
- Brown mustard

Instruction

1. Cut the french loaf in half. Place meats, cheese, lettuce, tomato, and onion on top.
2. Add mayo, brown mustard, salt, and pepper.
3. Slice into individual sandwiches. Makes 12 servings.

Super Bowl Sandwiches

Ingredients

- ½ lb. sliced Boar's Head turkey
- ½ cup coleslaw (make it yourself or buy from deli)
- 6 tbsp. Thousand Island dressing
- 4 plain bagels
- 4 slices provolone cheese

Instruction

1. Toast bagels.
2. Add all other ingredients to the toasted bagels. Makes 4 sandwiches.

Bagel Turkey Reuben

Ingredients

- 1 large tortilla (Mom uses lowfat spinach tortillas)
- 1 slice provolone cheese
- 3-4 slices Boar's Head turkey
- Shredded lettuce
- 5-6 thin cucumber slices
- 2 tbsp. tzatziki sauce (or hummus if you'd like)
- 2 tbsp. feta cheese

Instruction

1. Cut the french loaf in half. Place meats, cheese, lettuce, tomato, and onion on top.
2. Add mayo, brown mustard, salt, and pepper.
3. Slice into individual sandwiches. Makes 12 servings.

Spinach & Turkey Cheese Wrap

VEGETARIAN DISHES

Ingredients

- Olive oil
- 1 thick & lean London broil steak
- Pepper
- Cajun seasoning
- 1 package La Banderita® flour tortillas
- 1 yellow pepper, sliced into long strips
- 1 red pepper, sliced into long strips
- 1 sweet yellow onion, sliced into long strips
- ½ poblano pepper, diced
- Shredded cheese, if desired
- Med-hot salsa

Instruction

1. In a cast iron skillet, drizzle olive oil and heat on medium-high heat. Place onions, red and yellow peppers, and poblano peppers in the pan. Sauté until everything is browned. Do not burn.
2. Thoroughly season the steak with pepper and Cajun seasoning. Pat with a paper towel.
3. Place the steak on a hot grill (make sure it is really hot!) and cook for 3-4 minutes each side. When done, remove the steak and slice it into strips.
4. Serve steak strips and sautéed vegetables over a tortilla. Top with salsa and cheese.

Fajitas

Ingredients

- Aluminum foil
- Fresh broccoli
- Red skin potatoes
- Carrots, sliced
- Sweet yellow onion
- Olive oil
- Salt & pepper, to taste

Instruction

1. Place broccoli, potatoes, carrots, and onion in a sheet of foil. Drizzle with olive oil (or butter). Sprinkle with salt and pepper.
2. Turn grill on, heat to high heat, then reduce to medium. Loosely tighten pockets, then place the on the grill. Cook for 30-40 minutes.

Grilled Foiled Pockets
(Veggie Pockets)

Ingredients

- 1 large can black beans (with sauce)
- 1 garlic clove, minced or grated
- 1 tbsp. chili powder
- 2-3 shakes red pepper flakes
- 1 chicken bouillon cube, dissolved in ¼ cup hot water
- 1 sweet onion, diced
- ½ stick European butter (divided)
- ¼ poblano pepper, finely diced
- Mozzarella cheese (for topping, optional)

Instruction

1. Heat beans: warm black beans over medium heat, covered, until softened. Stir in garlic.
2. Season Beans: Add chili powder, red pepper flakes, and dissolved chicken bouillon. Stir well.
3. Sauté Aromatics: In a pan over medium-low heat, melt ¼ stick butter. Sauté onions until soft (but not clear).
4. Add Poblano & Butter: Add poblano pepper and remaining butter. Cook until everything softens and juices mix.
5. Combine & Simmer: Stir sautéed mixture into black beans and simmer on low for 20-30 minutes, stirring often.
6. Serve:
7. As a side dish: Sprinkle mozzarella on top.
8. As a burrito: Fill a warm tortilla with beans, shredded chicken, and lettuce.
9. As an egg roll filling: Mix with cooked chicken and corn, then bake.

Daniel's Black Beans

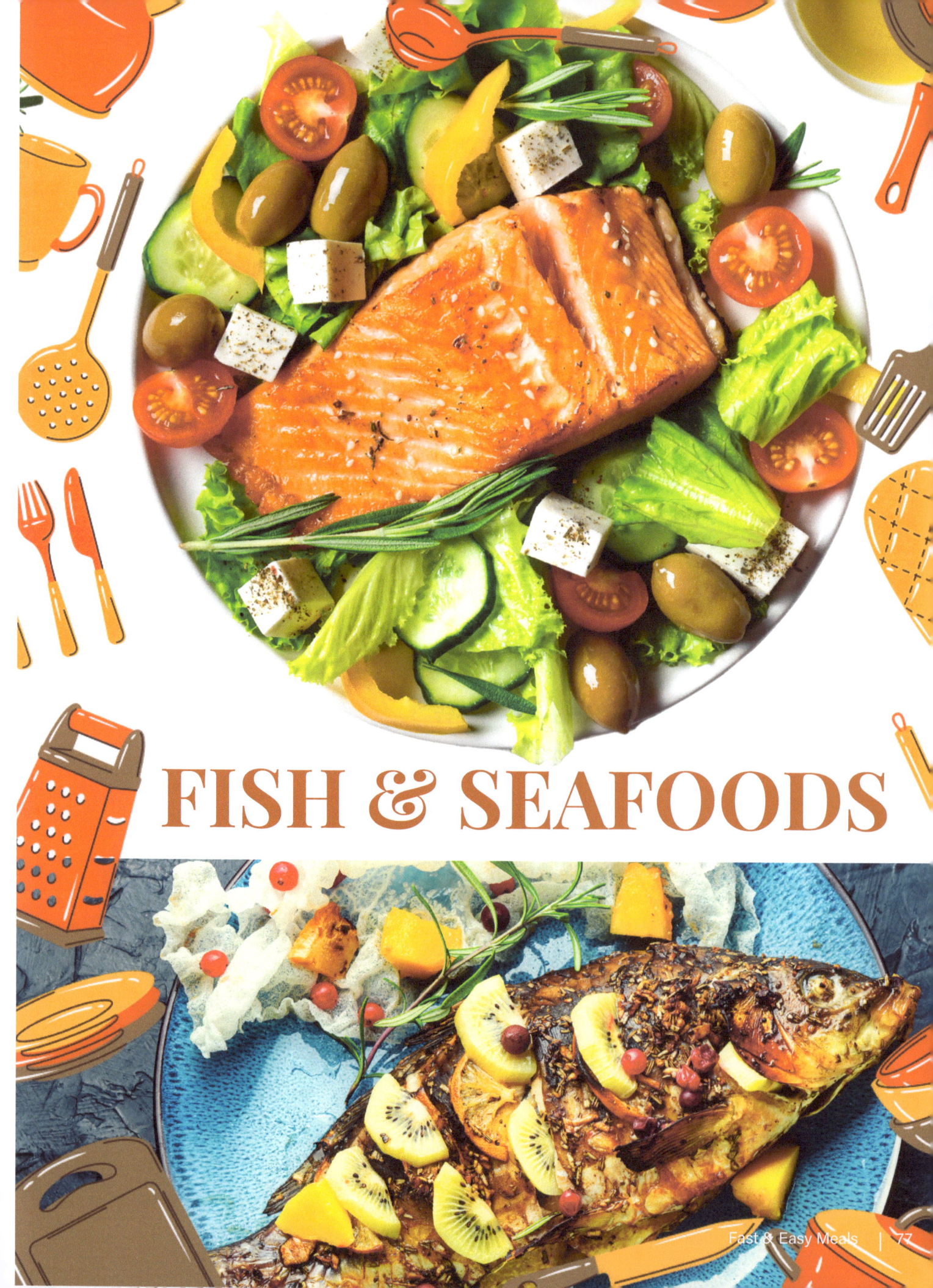

FISH & SEAFOODS

Ingredients

- Aluminum foil
- Butter or olive oil
- Salmon fillets
- Asparagus, cleaned & washed
- Lemon pepper seasoning

Instruction

1. Place and arrange salmon fillets and asparagus stalks in foil. Drizzle with butter or olive oil, and sprinkle with seasoning.
2. Turn grill on, heat to high heat, then reduce to medium. Place wrapped foil packets on the grill for about 30 minutes. (Check toward the end of cook time to see if the fillets are done. If not, adjust your time as needed.) Serve.

Grilled Foil Packets
(with Salmons)

Ingredients

- Trout
- 2 cups flour
- Lawry's® salt (or lemon pepper seasoning)
- Butter
- 1 large sweet yellow onion, sliced

Instruction

1. Clean and debone trout.
2. Put flour and salt or seasoning in a big plastic bag. (Be generous with your salt or seasoning.) Place fish in the bag and shake well.
3. In a large cast iron fry pan, heat butter on medium-low heat. Remove fish from the plastic bag and place it in the pan with butter. Add onions on top and fry, covered with a lid. Turn the fish over occasionally until it's browned well and the onions are done. Serve.

Wansten Family Rainbow Trout

(From Traverse City)

Ingredients

- 1 lb. fresh scallops
- 2 tbsp. flour
- Dash of salt & pepper
- 1 tsp. Lawry's® lemon pepper seasoning
- ¼ cup butter

Instruction

1. Thaw frozen scallops if they are not fresh. Rinse them thoroughly and pat them dry with a paper towel.
2. In a bowl, combine flour, salt, pepper, and lemon pepper seasoning. Dip the scallops into the seasoning mix to coat them.
3. In a skillet, melt butter. Add the seasoned scallops and cook them over medium heat, turning often, for 5 to 8 minutes or until they are browned and opaque in appearance.
4. Serve with lemon wedges and potatoes, or other vegetables.

Pan Fried Scallops

Ingredients

- Brine
- Corn on the cob, cut into halves
- Red skin potatoes, cut into 1-inch slices
- Lobster tails
- Shrimp
- 1 8 oz. bottle clam juice
- Garlic powder
- Lemon pepper seasoning
- 1 sweet yellow onion, diced
- Red pepper, sliced

Instruction

1. BRING THE BRINE WATER TO A BOIL. ADD CORN AND POTATOES FOR ABOUT 5 MINUTES. AFTER 5 MINUTES, REMOVE THE CORN AND POTATOES.
2. Put ¼ cup of brine water in the bottom of an oven pan. Place the corn and potatoes in the pan and arrange them neatly.
3. Cut the lobster tails along the back. Pull meat on top, and leave the tails connected.
4. Pour the lobster and shrimp into the pan. Be generous. Top with a full bottle of clam juice.
5. Season the contents of the pan with garlic powder and lemon pepper seasoning. Again, be generous, but don't kill it.
6. Add diced onion and sliced red pepper. (If desired, feel free to include orange and/or yellow peppers, clams, mussels, etc. too.)
7. Bake at 450° for 15-18 minutes, or until done.

Oven Seafood Bake

Ingredients

- 1 Cajun Andouille sausage, grilled and sliced at an angle
- 1 lb. shrimp, grilled with Cajun seasoning
- 1 cup instant rice (use slightly less water than package instructions)
- 1 can Cuban black beans (drain most liquid, leave some for flavor)
- 1 tbsp. medium restaurant salsa
- ½ cup queso cheese, heated
- 2 celery stalks, thinly sliced

Instruction

1. Grill the protein:
   - Grill Cajun Andouille sausage until browned. Slice at an angle.
   - Grill shrimp with Cajun seasoning until fully cooked.
2. Prepare the Rice:
   - Cook instant rice using slightly less water for a fluffy texture.
   - Before boiling, pour any sausage juice from the pan into the rice water for added flavor.
3. Mix Ingredients:
   - Stir black beans, salsa, and thinly sliced celery into the hot rice.
   - Add the sliced sausage and mix well.
4. Serve:
   - Plate the rice mixture, top with grilled shrimp, and drizzle heated queso cheese over the dish.

Rice and Beans with Cajun Shrimp & Sausage

TURKEY

Ingredients

- 14-19 lb. turkey
- Aluminum foil
- Canola oil
- 1 orange, cut into wedges
- 1 lemon, cut into wedges
- 1 onion, cut into wedges
- 6 sprigs rosemary
- 6 sprigs fresh sage
- 6 sprigs fresh oregano
- 7 tbsp. butter
- 2 tbsp. herbs de Provence
- 1 tbsp. olive oil
- 1½ tsp. fresh ground pepper
- 3 boxes chicken broth

Instruction

1. In a sink filled with cold water, thaw the turkey completely. (30 Minutes per 1 lb.)
2. Create a turkey triangle with aluminum foil and coat the part of the triangle that will touch the turkey with canola oil. Place the triangle on the turkey, and pat the exposed areas of the turkey with additional canola oil.
3. Place citrus in the turkey's cavity along with ½ of the fresh herbs. (Tip: take the orange and squeeze fresh juice inside the cavity.)
4. Mix butter, herbs de Provence, olive oil, and pepper in a separate bowl. Pour the mixture over the prepared turkey, then rub it underneath the skin and between the meat. Put more fresh sprigs into the bottom of the pan.
5. Let the prepared turkey marinate in the refrigerator overnight.
6. In the morning, cook the turkey at 500° for 15-20 minutes, then reduce heat to 350° and continue cooking for 13 minutes per pound. (A 19 lb. bird will cook for about 3-3 ½ hours.)
7. Baste the turkey continuously while baking with chicken broth and any leftover sprigs.

Turkey with Herbs de Provence & Citrus

CHICKEN

Ingredients

- Wings (Tip: Call the grocery store meat department and ask them to cut up about 100 drumettes (not the wing part, unless that is preferred). Mom & Dad get enough to freeze for later, sometimes upwards of 150-175 drumettes.)
- Pepper
- Vegetable oil

Best Wings Ever

Instruction

1. Preheat the oven to 400°. Grease cookie sheets or shallow pans with vegetable oil.
2. Place the wings and drums on the greased trays. Season them with pepper.
3. Place the baking sheets in the oven for 45 minutes. When they are done and cooled, place them in a freezer bag. (Tip: Portion out individual servings with 5 drums per bag.)
4. When you want to serve the wings, put the oven on broil and remove the bags from the freezer. Place the wings into the oven for 5-7 minutes per side.
5. Serve the wings with Kraft® ranch, Sweet Baby Ray's® Hickory and Brown Sugar BBQ Sauce, or Terry Ho's™ Yum Yum Light Sauce. (Your choice based on flavor.)

Ingredients

- Milk
- 1½ cups flour
- 2½ tbsp. Lawry's® seasoning
- ½ tsp. finely ground pepper
- Vegetable oil or butter

Instruction

1. Heat vegetable oil or butter in a pan. (Tip: mom prefers butter, just don't burn it.)
2. Rinse the chicken breasts in water. Pat them dry with a paper towel. (Tip: This is the secret to the batter not falling off.)
3. Dip the chicken breasts in the egg mixture, then coat them with flour. Put the breasts into the pan with the butter or vegetable oil. Brown the breasts on both sides, then turn the heat down to medium-low heat for 30 minutes. Serve.

Mom's Fried Chicken

Ingredients

- 2 cups chicken broth
- ⅔ cup long grain rice
- 3 tbsp. butter
- 3 tbsp. all purpose flour
- 1½ tsp. salt
- Dash of pepper
- 2 cups milk
- 2 cubs cubed chicken (use dark meat)
- 1 10 oz. package frozen chopped broccoli, cooked & drained
- 1 4oz. can sliced mushrooms, drained
- Shredded cheddar cheese, mild

Instruction

1. In a saucepan, bring chicken broth and rice to a boil. Simmer and cover for 15 minutes.
2. Remove the rice from heat. Let stand covered for 10 minutes.
3. In a separate pan, melt the butter, then stir in flour, salt, and pepper. Add milk. Cook and stir until bubbly.
4. Stir in cubed chicken, cooked rice, broccoli, and mushrooms.
5. Pour the mixture into a casserole dish and mix in some shredded cheese. Be sure to top the casserole with cheese as well.
6. Bake, covered, at 350° for 30-35 minutes. Cool and serve.

Mom's Chicken Broccoli Bake

Ingredients

- 4 skinless, boneless chicken breasts
- 1 jar Barilla® basil & tomato sauce
- 1 package shredded mozzarella cheese
- Vegetable oil

Instruction

1. Preheat the oven to 350°. In a fry pan with vegetable oil, brown the chicken breasts on both sides.
2. When the breasts are browned nicely, put them in a baking dish. Pour the tomato sauce over the chicken, top with cheese, and bake for 30-40 minutes. Cool and serve.

Paleo Chicken Breast

Ingredients

- 6 chicken thighs
- Tony Chachere's creole seasoning

Paleo
Chicken

Instruction

1. Put the chicken thighs in a large fry pan. Lightly season thighs with the creole seasoning on just one side.
2. Turn the stove on high heat. Brown the thighs well on both sides with a lid on.
3. Turn the heat down to medium/ medium-low and fry the thighs for about 30 minutes, or until done. Serve with veggies.

Ingredients

- 3 lbs. chicken, cut up. (Use 4 thighs and 4 legs)
- 1 large onion, sliced
- 1 16 oz. can organic diced tomatoes
- 1 8 oz. can organic tomato sauce
- 1 cup sliced mushrooms
- 2-3 cloves garlic, diced
- 2 tsp. fresh oregano
- ½ tsp. fresh basil, diced
- 1 bay leaf
- ¼ cup dry white wine
- Salt & pepper, to taste

Instruction

1. Place onion on the bottom of a slow cooker. Add chicken, tomato sauce, and diced tomatoes.
2. Chop the mushrooms and add them to the slow cooker. On top of the mushrooms, add the garlic, oregano, and basil.
3. Add the bay leaf, wine, salt, and pepper to your liking.
4. Cover and cook on medium-high heat for 4-6 hours. Serve.

Easy Chicken Cacciatore

Chicken 'N' Dumplings

Ingredients

For Chicken:
- 5-6 lb. ready-to-cook stewing chicken. (Tip: you can cut the chicken up if you'd like, but Mom & Dad use the whole chicken.)
- 2 sprigs parsley
- 4 celery branches, diced
- 1 carrot, pared & sliced
- 1 small sweet yellow onion, cut up
- 2 tsp. salt
- ½ tsp. pepper

For Dumplings:
- 1 cup all purpose flour, sifted
- 2 tsp. baking powder
- ½ tsp. salt
- ½ cup milk
- 2 tbsp. salad oil
- Gravy from chicken
- 1 package mixed vegetables

Instruction

1. Chicken:
   - Rinse chicken cavity, place in a large pot with 2 quarts of water and remaining ingredients. Cover, boil, then simmer for 2½ hours until tender. Keep chicken in broth.
2. Dumplings:
   - Mix flour, baking powder, and salt. Combine milk and oil, then add to dry ingredients. Drop spoonfuls into boiling broth over chicken. Cover and cook for 12-15 minutes.
3. Gravy:
   - Mix flour and milk until smooth. Pour into boiling broth, add vegetables, and stir until thickened. Serve over chicken and dumplings.

Ingredients

- 1 5-6 lb. whole chicken
- ½ cup butter
- 1 tbsp. salt
- 1 tsp. black pepper
- ½ cup tarragon, chopped
- 1 cup chicken broth
- 2 lemons, juiced
- 1 shallot, finely chopped

Instruction

1. Preheat the oven to 425°. Wash the chicken inside and out. Pat it dry with a paper towel. Season the chicken with salt and pepper.
2. Melt ¼ cup butter and add half of the chopped herbs.
3. With your fingers, gently work the butter and herb mixture underneath the skin, breast, and thigh of the chicken. Don't break the skin! Cover the outside of the chicken skin as well. Place the chicken into a roasting pan.
4. In a saucepan, bring shallots, lemon juice, and chicken broth to a boil.
5. Roast the chicken for 20 minutes, then reduce heat to 400°.
6. Baste the chicken with the broth mixture every 15 minutes, and roast it for the remaining 5 minutes or until the inside temperature reaches 165°. (Tip: Mom usually roasts for about 1 more hour, but just continue checking the temperature.)
7. Make gravy with the rest of the juice.
8. Cool the chicken after removing it from the oven. Serve with potatoes or other veggies.

Easy Herbed Roasted Chicken

Ingredients

- 3-4 boneless, skinless chicken breasts
- 1 can cream of chicken soup
- 2-3 tsp. chicken bouillon granules
- Cornstarch with water to thicken gravy (about 3 tbsp. is best, but you can adjust based on preferred thickness)
- ⅛ tsp. ground pepper

Instruction

1. Place chicken in the bottom of a slow cooker. Add bouillon, 2 cups of water, cream of chicken soup, and pepper. Cover tightly and place slow cooker on high. Cook for 8 hours, stirring occasionally.
2. After 8 hours, mix the cornstarch with 1 cup of water and make sure all lumps are removed. Stir the chicken, then add the cornstarch mixture into the slow cooker to thicken for gravy. It is best if the meat is shredded, but this is your choice.
3. Add a frozen package of mixed veggies if you desire. Serve over mashed potatoes, rice, or noodles.

Slow Cooker Chicken & Gravy

Ingredients

- 6 chicken thighs
- 4 chicken legs
- Lawry's® seasoned salt
- 4-6 potatoes, with skin on
- 1 bag mixed vegetables

Instruction

1. Place chicken on a baking sheet. Lightly sprinkle the chicken with Lawry's® seasoning.
2. Bake at 350°, along with whole potatoes, for 1 hour and 15-20 minutes. Serve with mixed vegetables.

Lazy Day Dinner

Ingredients

- Chicken thighs, legs, and breasts,cut up with skin on
- 2 cans condensed milk (punchholes on both sides for easypouring)
- Salt & pepper, to taste
- Paprika
- Lawry's® seasoned salt
- Vegetable oil

Instruction

1. Put just enough vegetable oil into a deep-dish cast iron skillet or electric frying pan to cover the bottom of the pan. Heat the oil, but don't get it too hot that it's smoking.
2. Take completely thawed chicken and lightly sprinkle it with Lawry's® on both sides. Place chicken in the try pan and turn down to low heat. Cook, turning chicken over frequently.
3. When the chicken is almost done, pour condensed milk into the pan and add salt and pepper. Scrape the bottom of the pan to lift the chicken and cook it in the milk for about 30-40 minutes. Serve topped with paprika and with peas on the side.

Grama Rose's Milk Gravy Chicken

Ingredients

- 6 chicken thighs
- 4 chicken legs
- Lawry's® seasoned salt
- 4-6 potatoes, with skin on
- 1 bag mixed vegetables

Instruction

1. Cook bacon. Turn heat on/off as needed don't over cook save grease to fry chicken.
2. Cook pasta in lightly salted water
3. Microwave peas in bag 5min
4. Open a large can of diced tomatoes. And drain all liquid
5. When pasta is done, drain.
6. Add bread crumbs to all sides of the chicken. Cook in hot bacon grease until brown on all sides.
7. heat tomatoes 4cheese sauce and pees and bacon broken into 1/2 inch sizes. Add 1pinch crushed dried red peppers. spread over top of sauce
8. 8. Stir sauce add another pinch of dried red peppers cook 10 minutes to marinate

Bacon Chicken Cavatappi

PORK

Ingredients

- 1 large pork loin, unseasoned
- Lawry's® lemon pepper seasoning
- Chicken bouillon
- Olive oil

Lemon Pepper Roast

Instruction

1. Preheat the oven to 375°. Place the pork loins on aluminum foil. Pour olive oil all over the roast (the loins seal in the juices well), then sprinkle lemon pepper all over the roast.
2. Seal the marinated pork loins in aluminum foil and place them in a baking dish. Place the dish in the oven and cook for 1 hour and 15 minutes. Serve with mashed potatoes (use juices from the roast to make lemon pepper chicken bouillon gravy) and mixed veggies.

Ingredients

- 1 5 lb. boneless pork top roast (double loin tied)
- ¾ cup dry red wine
- ⅓ cup packed brown sugar
- ¼ cup vinegar
- ¼ cup ketchup
- ¼ cup water
- 2 tbsp. cooking oil
- 1 tbsp. soy sauce
- 1 clove garlic, minced
- 1 tsp. curry powder
- ½ tsp. ground ginger
- ¼ tsp. black pepper
- 2 tsp. cornstarch
- Carrots, whole with leaves left on
- 3 large beets with leafy stems attached
- Quartered potatoes, if desired

Festive Pork Roast

Instruction

1. PLACE THE ROAST IN A LARGE PLASTIC BAG. SET IN A DEEP BOWL.
2. For the marinade, combine wine, brown sugar, vinegar, ketchup, water, oil, soy sauce, garlic, curry powder, ginger, and pepper.
3. Pour the marinade over the meat in the bag. Seal and marinate in the refrigerator for 6-8 hours, turning the meat in the bag several times to evenly coat the roast.
4. After marinating, drain the meat. Reserve, cover, and chill 1¼ cup of the marinade. Pat the meat dry with paper towels.
5. Arrange the roast in a roasting pan. Add beets and carrots (remember to keep the leaves on!). Pour the marinade over the meat and vegetables for basting. Roast, uncovered, at 325° for 2¼ hours, basting with marinade occasionally. When done, make gravy with the drippings. Serve with mashed potatoes.

SAUSAGE

Ingredients

- 1 lb. lean ground beef
- 1 lb. Jimmy Dean® sausage
- 2 cloves fresh garlic, minced
- 1 tbsp. sweet yellow onion, diced
- 2 jars Bertolli® Basil & Tomato Sauce
- 5-6 zucchinis, thinly sliced the long way to resemble noodles
- 2 cups fresh grated parmesan or mozzarella cheese

Instruction

1. Lay one level of meat sauce, cheese, and zucchini noodles in a pan. Repeat until all layers are complete.
2. Bake in oven at 350° for 30 minutes.

Paleo Zucchini Lasagna

Ingredients

- 1 lb. Jimmy Dean® Italian sausage
- 1 jar Barilla® Basil & Tomato Spaghetti sauce
- 2 lbs. regular spaghetti noodles, uncooked

Instruction

1. Brown the sausage in a pan until it is cooked well. Drain and add the spaghetti sauce. Turn heat down to a simmer.
2. Cook the spaghetti noodles according to the directions on the box. Drain and add butter for flavor. Serve with sausage sauce.

Family's Favorite Spaghetti

Mom & Dad's note: #1 favorite family recipe!

BEEF

Ingredients

- 2 lbs. lean ground beef
- 1 sweet yellow onion
- 2 oz. cans tomato sauce
- 1 cup ketchup
- ½ cup brown sugar
- 2 tsp. mustard
- 2 cloves garlic, minced
- 3 tbsp. Worcestershire sauce
- Salt & pepper, to taste
- Hamburger buns

Instruction

1. Brown the ground beef. Place it in a slow cooker with remaining ingredients (except buns) on medium heat.
2. Cook for 3-4 hours. Serve on buns.

Slow Cooker Sloppy Joes

Ingredients

- 2 lbs. ground beef
- 1 lb. Jimmy Dean® sausage
- 3 celery stalks, diced
- 1 sweet yellow onion, diced
- 2 carrots, diced
- 3 eggs
- ½ cup almond meal
- 2 tbsp. dried oregano
- 1 tbsp. garlic powder
- Pinch of cayenne pepper
- Dash of salt & pepper
- 2 jars Bertolli® tomato & basil sauce

Instruction

1. Mix all ingredients (except tomato sauce) together in a large bowl. Form the meat mixture into individual meatballs, then place them in the bottom of a slow cooker. Cook until browned.
2. When the meatballs are browned and cooked, drain them and put them back into the cooker. Add tomato and basil sauce. Heat for 1 hour and serve.

Paleo Meatballs

THIS RECIPE IS INSPIRED BY CHEF JOHN'S CLASSIC MEATBALLS FOR SPAGHETTI WITH RED SAUCE. WHILE I'VE ADDED MY OWN TWIST, FULL CREDIT GOES TO CHEF JOHN FOR THE ORIGINAL CREATION. CLICH HERE FOR HIS ORIGINAL RECIPE.

Ingredients

- 2 lbs. extra lean ground beef
- 1-2 cloves garlic, chopped
- 1 tsp. basil, chopped
- 1 can tomato paste
- ½ cup ketchup
- 1 tbsp. mustard
- 4-6 eggs
- ¼ onion, chopped

Instruction

1. Mix all ingredients (except ketchup) together. Place the mixture into a loaf pan and drizzle the top with ketchup.
2. Bake at 350° for 1 hour and 20 minutes.

Paleo Meatloaf

Ingredients

- 1 boneless chuck roast (pick the most lean one)
- 1 bag pearl onions (in the freezer section)
- 1 lb. bag baby carrots
- 5 lb. bag red skin potatoes
- 1-2 packages Lipton® dry beefy mushroom soup, for seasoning
- Cornstarch

Instruction

1. Place the roast in a crockpot. Rinse the onions, carrots, and potatoes well, then add them to the crockpot. Top with lipton® seasoning and 2 cups of water.
2. Seal the crockpot and cook on high for 5-6 hours. Toward the end of cooking, add water and cornstarch to create gravy. Serve.

Pot Roast

Ingredients

- 1 4-5 lb. lean chuck roast
- 1 clove fresh garlic, chopped
- 1-2 packages fresh mushrooms, sliced
- 1 can beefy mushroom soup
- Salt & pepper, to taste
- 2½ tbsp. beef bouillon (or to taste)
- Cornstarch

Instruction

1. Place roast on the bottom of a slow cooker. Add salt, pepper, garlic, and mushrooms. Pour 2 ½ cups water in, along with bouillon. Cover tightly and cook on high for 8 hours.
2. After 8 hours, stir and add the cornstarch with water mixture to thicken for gravy. (Tip: It is best if the beef is a bit shredded.)
3. Thicken the gravy. If you would like, you can add a bag of mixed vegetables in as well. Serve over mashed potatoes, rice, or noodles.

Slow Cooker Beef & Gravy

Ingredients

- 2 lbs. round steak, cubed or cut into strips
- All purpose flour
- 2 tbsp. olive oil
- 2 tbsp. butter
- 1 medium sweet onion
- 8-16 oz. fresh mushrooms, sliced
- 1 10¾ oz. can beef broth
- 1 10¾ oz. can cream of mushroom soup
- Salt & pepper, to taste
- 1 cup sour cream
- Egg noodles

Instruction

1. Season the steak strips with salt and pepper, then dust them with flour.
2. In a large skillet, quickly brown the strips on both sides in olive oil and butter. Remove them from the pan.
3. Add the onion slices and mushrooms to the pan. Sauté them in the steak drippings for a few minutes until the onions are tender. Sprinkle the vegetables with 1 tsp. flour.
4. Put the steak back into the pan with the onions and mushrooms. Add the mushroom soup and beef broth. Cook over low heat for about 30 minutes, covered.
5. Adjust the seasoning to your preferred taste, adding salt and pepper as needed. Stir in the sour cream during the last few minutes, right before you are preparing to serve. Serve over cooked egg noodles.

Beef Stroganoff

Ingredients

- Lean burger patties
- Salad (any way you desire)

Instruction

1. Grill burger patties. Place them on top of your choice of salad and add your preferred dressing. Serve.

Paleo Burger Bundles

Ingredients

- 6-12 skewers
- 1½ lb. beef sirloin, cut into 1-inch cubes
- 2 chicken breasts, cut into 1-inch cubes
- 1 package whole, fresh mushrooms, rinsed & cleaned
- 1 sweet yellow onion, cut into wedges
- 1 yellow bell pepper, cut into 2-inch cubes
- 1 red bell pepper, cut into 2-inch cubes
- Lawry's® marinade (Tip: mesquite is great, but you can choose your seasoning based on preference.)

Instruction

1. Preheat the grill and place on medium-high heat.
2. Start to prepare the kebobs by putting one cube of chicken, one cube of steak, then a few cubes of vegetables on a skewer. Repeat until each skewer is full.
3. Place skewers on a baking dish and pour the marinade over each of them. When the grill is ready, place the skewers on the grill and turn them over every 5 minutes, or until each one is done. (This generally takes about 20-25 minutes.) Serve with corn on the cob.

Mom's Grilled KEbAb's (Marinated)

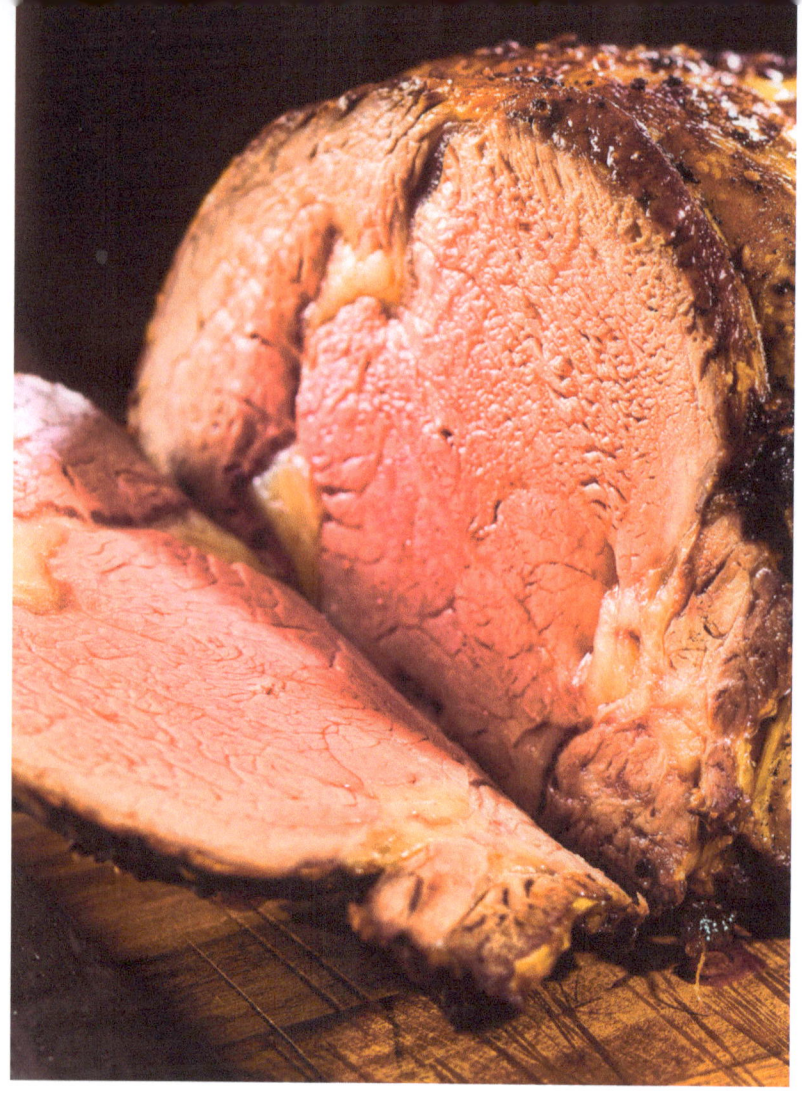

Ingredients

For Rub:
- ½ cup fresh chopped parsley
- ½ cup fresh chopped rosemary
- ½ cup fresh chopped tarragon
- ¼ cup fresh chopped thyme
- 2 tbsp. salt
- 2 garlic cloves, pressed
- ½ cup extra virgin olive oil

For Roast:
- 1 10-12 lb. prime rib roast (keep it at room temperature)

Instruction

1. Mix all of the rub ingredients together with a wire whisk. Apply the rub to the exterior of the entire roast.
2. For Roast:
   - Preheat the oven to 325°. Put the roast in a roasting pan and keep it uncovered.
   - Cook the roast for 1½ hours, or until the internal temperature is 120°. Serve with drippings from the pan.

Prime Rib With Rub

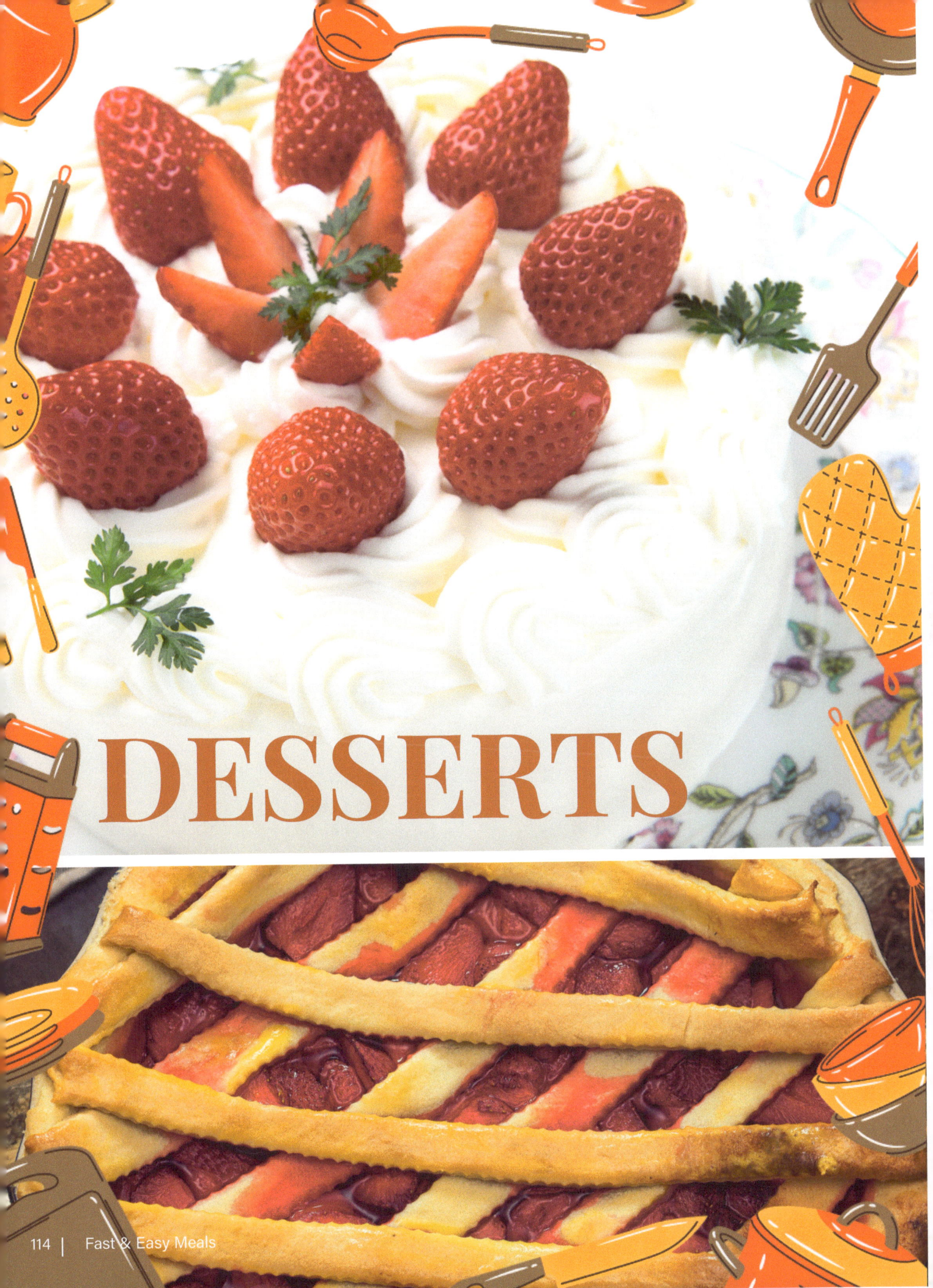

DESSERTS

Ingredients

- 1 large package orange Jell-O®
- 1 can fruit cocktail, drained
- ½ can crushed pineapple, drained
- Cool Whip

Instruction

1. Prepare the jell-o according to directions on the box. Pour the drained fruit into the jell-o and mix.
2. Pour the Jell-O into a mold or decorative clear dish. Refrigerate according to instructions on the Jell-O box, plus 1 additional hour. Serve with Cool Whip.

Fruit Jell-O

Ingredients

- 2 20 oz. cans Dole® crushed pineapple
- 1 16 oz. tub Cool Whip

Instruction

1. Drain juice from the pineapple. Place the pineapple into a bowl.
2. Add Cool Whip in with the pineapple and mix everything together. Seal the edge and cover the mix with more Cool Whip.
3. Cover and chill in the refrigerator for 24 hours. Serve

Angie's Pineapple Dessert

Ingredients

- Apples, with skins left on, cut in half, and cores removed
- Butter
- Brown sugar
- Cinnamon

Instruction

1. Preheat the oven to 350°. Take halved, cored apples and place them on a baking sheet. Put a dab of butter in each apple.
2. Sprinkle apples with brown sugar and cinnamon. Place them in the oven and bake for 30-40 minutes. Serve.

Cinnamon Baked Apples

Ingredients

For Crust:
- 2 cups sifted all purpose flour
- 1 tsp. salt
- ⅔ cup shortening
- 5-7 tbsp. cold water

For Filling:
- 6-8 tart apples, pared, cored, and thinly sliced (If the apples lack tartness, add 1 tbsp. lemon juice)
- ¾-1 cup sugar
- 2 tbsp. all purpose flour
- ½-1 tsp. ground cinnamon
- Dash of nutmeg
- 2 tbsp. butter

Apple Pie

Instruction

For crust:
1. Add flour, salt, and shortening to a large mixing bowl. Cut the shortening into the flour until it is in small pieces. Sprinkle water in, a bit at a time, until the crust is moist.
2. Form the crust into a ball. Cut it in half and roll each half out with a rolling pin. Place one half of the crust into a 9-inch pie pan and flute the edges. Cover and set aside.

For Filling:
3. Combine all filling ingredients together. Pour the filling on top of the previously prepared pie pastry. Dot with butter.
4. Top with the second half of the pie pastry, cutting slits for steam to escape. Seal the edges of the pie crusts together and sprinkle the top with sugar, just to make it pretty.
5. Bake at 400° for 50 minutes, or until done. Cool and serve.

Ingredients

- 1 9-inch pie shell
- 1 quart fresh strawberries
- ¾ cup sugar
- 2 tbsp. cornstarch
- ⅛ tsp. salt
- 1 cup water
- 4 tbsp. strawberry gelatin
- 1½ tsp. lemon juice
- ½ tsp. vanilla
- Whipped topping

Strawberry Pie

Instruction

1. Bake the pie shell according to the package instructions.
2. Wash, stem, and cut the strawberries in half and set them aside.
3. In a small saucepan, combine sugar, cornstarch, salt, and water. Cook over medium heat, stirring constantly for 8-10 minutes, or until the mixture turns clear, thick, and bubbly.
4. Remove from heat and stir in gelatin, lemon juice, and vanilla. Cook for 5 minutes. Fold the berries in and pour the mixture into a pie shell. Chill for 4 hours or overnight.

Ingredients

- 1 angel food cake
- 2-3 quarts fresh strawberries
- 2-3 packages Splenda

Instruction

1. Cut the strawberries and place them in a mixing bowl. Take a wire whisk and chop the strawberries until there is juice in the bowl, but leave some chunks of strawberries.
2. Add Splenda to the bowl. Mix, then chill for 2 hours. Serve over angel food cake.

Lite Strawberry Shortcake

Ingredients

- 6 tbsp. butter
- ¾ cup cornstarch or 1½ cups flour
- 2¼ cup sugar
- 1 tsp. salt
- 1½ quart milk (6 cups)
- 6 eggs, beaten
- 1 tbsp. vanilla extract
- 1 tbsp. almond extract

Cooked Custard

Instruction

1. Melt the butter. Blend in the cornstarch (or flour), sugar, and salt. Gradually bring to a boil on a medium flame. When boiling, slowly start to add the milk.
2. When the milk is added, turn down to low heat and stir in the beaten eggs. Cook for 2 minutes, stirring constantly.
3. Remove from heat, then add vanilla and almond extract. Mix, cool, and serve.

Ingredients

- 1 package instant vanilla pudding
- 1 package instant chocolate pudding
- 1 package instant pistachio pudding
- Fresh blackberries
- Fresh raspberries
- Fresh strawberries
- 1 tub Cool Whip

Instruction

1. In a clear, tall glass dessert dish, layer pudding: chocolate, vanilla, pistachio.
2. Add Cool Whip and seal the edges, smoothing the top.
3. Top with berries. Chill for 2 hours and serve.

Triple Layer Pudding Dessert

Ingredients

- 1 package Oreo cookies
- 1 gallon vanilla ice cream (premium brand)
- 1 package semi-sweet chocolate chips, melted
- 1 stick European butter

Instruction

1. Put crumbled oreos into a large square dish. Mix in a stick of butter.
2. Add the gallon of ice cream into the dish. Mix. Smooth the top with a spatula.
3. Drizzle the melted chocolate chips on top. Freeze and serve.

Oreo Ice Cream Dessert

Ingredients

- 4 cups granulated sugar
- 14½ oz. can evaporated milk
- 1 cup butter
- 12 oz. package semi-sweet chocolate chips
- 7 oz. jar marshmallow crème
- 1 tsp. vanilla
- 1 cup chopped walnuts

Remarkable Fudge

Instruction

1. Grease all sides of a heavy 3-quart saucepan. Add sugar, evaporated milk, and butter into the pan. Cook over medium heat until the mixture forms into a soft ball, stirring often.
2. Remove from heat. Stir in the chocolate chips until they are melted. (Tip: Chocolate baking bars for making fudge are found in the baking section.)
3. Stir in marshmallow, vanilla, and walnuts. Beat the fudge until the chocolate is fully melted. Pour into the buttered pan and score while still warm. Cool and serve.

Ingredients

- 1 cup softened butter
- 1½ cup sugar
- 2 eggs
- 1 tsp. vanilla
- 2¾ cups flour
- 2 tsp. cream of tartar
- 1 tsp. baking soda
- ½ tsp. salt
- 3 tbsp. sugar
- 1 tbsp. cinnamon

Instruction

1. Preheat the oven to 400°. In a large mixing bowl, mix sugar, flour, cream of tartar, baking soda, and salt in with butter, eggs, and vanilla.
2. In a separate bowl, mix sugar and cinnamon. Set aside.
3. Roll the dough from step. 1 into 1-inch balls and dip them into the cinnamon and sugar mix. Place the dough balls on a cookie sheet and bake for 8-10 minutes. Cool and serve.

Snickerdoodles

Ingredients

- 1 stick butter
- 2 cups sugar
- ½ cup milk
- ¼ cup cocoa
- 1 cup peanut butter
- 2 tsp. vanilla
- 3 cups quick oats
- ¼ tsp. salt

Instruction

1. Line a baking sheet with wax paper. In a small saucepan over medium-high heat, whisk together butter, sugar, milk, and cocoa. Bring to a boil for 1-2 minutes. Remove from heat.
2. Whisk in peanut butter and vanilla. Blend well. Pour in oats and stir.
3. On a tablespoon, shape dough into small balls and drop them one at a time onto the wax paper. Let cool. Chill for 1 hour and serve.

Chocolate Peanut Butter No Bake

Ingredients

- 2½ cups all purpose flour
- 1 tsp. baking soda
- 1 tsp. baking powder
- 1 cup melted butter
- ½ tsp. salt
- ¾ cup sugar
- 1 cup brown sugar
- 2 eggs
- 1 tsp. vanilla
- 2 cups semi-sweet chocolate chips
- Chopped nuts (optional)

Instruction

1. Preheat the oven to 350°. Mix all ingredients together until dough forms.
2. Shape the dough into balls and place them on a cookie sheet. Bake for 8-10 minutes. Serve.

Best Chocolate Chip Cookies Ever

Ingredients

For Cookies:
• ⅓ cup shortening
• ⅓ cup sugar
• 1 egg
• ⅔ cup honey
• 1 tsp. salt
• 1 tsp. baking soda
• 2¾ cups flour

For Frosting:
• 1 lb. confectioners sugar (2 cups)
• ½ cup butter, softened
• 1½ tsp. vanilla extract
• 2 tbsp. mix

Instruction

For cookies:
1. Combine all ingredients, shape into balls, and bake on a cookie sheet at 375° for 10 minutes. Serves 1 dozen.

For Frosting:
2. Mix all ingredients with a mixer on high. Add colors based on preference.

Best "Grama's Christmas Cookie Recipe" with Frosting

Ingredients

- 2 eggs
- 2¼ tsp. baking powder
- 2 cups brown sugar
- 2½ cups flour
- ½ tsp. salt
- 1 cup semi-sweet chocolate chips
- 1 tsp. vanilla
- 1½ cups graham cracker crumbs
- ½ cup unsalted butter
- ⅔ cup salted butter
- 1 cup mini marshmallows
- ½ cup regular marshmallows
- 1 milk chocolate candy bar

Instruction

1. Preheat the oven to 325°. Grease a 9x13 nonstick pan.
2. Mix butter and graham cracker crumbs with a fork. Press the mixture down into the baking dish and set aside.
3. In a large bowl, mix butter, sugar, eggs, and vanilla.
4. In a separate bowl, mix flour, baking powder, and salt. Pour the dry mixture into the liquid mixture. Fold in the chocolate chips and marshmallows.
5. Pour the combined mixture on top of the crust and spread evenly. Bake for 30-40 minutes. Cool and enjoy!

S'more Bars

Ingredients

For Topping:
- ¼ cup brown sugar
- 1 tbsp. flour
- 1 tsp. ground cinnamon
- 1 tbsp. melted butter
- ½ cup chopped nuts (optional)

For Cake:
- ¼ cup vegetable oil
- 1 egg, beaten
- ½ cup milk
- 1½ cups sifted flour
- ¾ cup sugar
- 2 tsp. baking powder
- ½ tsp. salt

Instruction

For topping:
1. Mix all ingredients together.

For Cake:
2. In a large bowl, mix all ingredients together well. Pour the mixture into a greased 9x9x2-inch pan. Sprinkle with topping.
3. Bake at 375° for 25 minutes. Cool and serve.

Homemade Coffee Cake

Ingredients

- 5¾-6¼ cups all purpose flour
- 1 package active dry yeast
- 2¼ cups milk
- 2 tbsp. sugar
- 1 tbsp. shortening
- 2 tsp. salt

Instruction

1. In a large mixing bowl, combine flour and yeast. In a saucepan, heat milk, sugar, shortening, and salt until warm, stirring constantly until shortening almost melts.
2. Add the liquid mixture to the dry mixture. Beat with an electric mixture at low speed for 30 seconds, scraping the sides of the bowl constantly. Increase to high speed and beat for an additional 3 minutes. By hand, stir in enough of the remaining flour to make a moderately stiff dough, Turn out the dough onto a lightly floured surface and knead it until it's smooth and elastic, or about 8-10 minutes. Then shape the dough into a ball.
3. Place the dough into a lightly greased bowl and turn it once to coat. Cover and let it rise in a warm place until it doubles in size, or about 1¼ hours. After the dough has risen, punch it down and turn it again onto a lightly floured service. Divide it in half. Shape both halves into smooth balls. Cover and let them rest for 10 minutes.
4. Shape the dough balls into loaves and place them into greased loaf pans. Cover and let them rise in a warm place until they double in size, or about 45-60 minutes.
5. Bake the loaves at 375° for about 45 minutes, or until done. If the tops brown too quickly, cover them with foil for the last 15 minutes. Makes 2 loaves.

Homemade Bread

Ingredients

- 1 ½ cups whole milk
- ½ cup granulated sugar
- 3 ½ tablespoons cornstarch
- 4 egg yolks
- 2 tablespoons butter
- 2 teaspoons vanilla extract

Instruction

1. Heat the milk & sugar: in a saucepan over medium heat, combine the milk and sugar. Stir occasionally until the sugar dissolves and the mixture is warm (but not boiling).
2. Prepare the Egg Mixture: In a separate bowl, whisk together the cornstarch and egg yolks until smooth.
3. Temper the Eggs: Slowly add a small amount of the warm milk mixture into the egg mixture while whisking continuously. This prevents the eggs from scrambling.
4. Combine & Cook: Pour the tempered egg mixture back into the saucepan with the remaining milk. Cook over low to medium heat, stirring constantly, until the mixture thickens to a pudding-like consistency.
5. Add Butter & Vanilla: Remove the saucepan from heat and stir in the butter and vanilla extract until fully incorporated.
6. Chill & Serve: Pour the custard into serving dishes, cover with plastic wrap (to prevent skin from forming), and refrigerate until set. Serve chilled and enjoy!

Vanilla Custard Pudding (high protein)